CARGO LINERS AND TRAMPS

D1556498

Mark Lee Inman

AMBERLEY

To Pud.

A gracious wife is more precious than rubies.
(τιμιωτέρα δε εστί λικῶν πολυτελῶν η τοιαύτη) *(Prov. 31:10 LXX)*

First published 2018

Amberley Publishing
The Hill, Stroud
Gloucestershire, GL5 4EP

www.amberleybooks.com

British Library Cataloguing in Publication Data.
A catalogue record for this book is available from the British Library.

ISBN 978 1 4456 7384 4 (print)
ISBN 978 1 4456 7385 1 (ebook)

Typesetting and Origination by Amberley Publishing.
Printed in Great Britain.

Contents

Introduction

Most people when confronted with the term 'liner' will immediately think of a magnificent ship carrying passengers in great style and luxury on a regular service from Europe to North America, South Africa or the Far East and Australia. Key to the understanding of the word 'liner' is the regular service such as that operated by the famous Cunard 'Queens', who ran a regular weekly service across the North Atlantic, or the Union-Castle weekly mail service to South Africa. Such ships were relatively large, primarily carried passengers and usually had a mail contract. Cargo capacity was limited.

Forming what might be called the second division were cargo liners. These also operated a regular scheduled service but with the priority being cargo and very few passengers. These ships were much smaller than the passenger liners and form most of the pictures in this collection.

By contrast, tramps carried cargo wherever they were required to.

Most of the pictures in this collection are official company postcards or official company photographs. In my early teens, the number of ships calling at the Bristol Channel ports was limited. To supplement one's knowledge and interest, I embarked on an exercise to ask the shipping companies for photographs of their ships, particularly the ones I was unlikely to see. Most responded, and some were very generous, so a substantial collection was built up.

A few photographs are included from my own efforts with my trusty Voigtlander Vito C. They have given me the opportunity to show off efforts in other ports around the UK and Continental Europe. In some cases I have supplemented knowledge by showing how shipping companies responded to the changing demands of the 1960s.

The companies are listed alphabetically. Each caption contains a brief history of the company and the individual ship.

In carrying out the research, I am indebted to H. M. Le Fleming's *Ships of the Holland-America Line*, Laurence Dunn's *Ships of the Union Castle Line*, my trusted and venerated copies of Bert Moody's *Ocean Ships*, Moss and Hume's *Shipbuilders to the World*, C. H. Milsom's two-volume *Blue Funnels in the Mersey*, Ambrose Greenway's *Cargo Liners*, Andrew Wiltshire's *Looking Back at Traditional Cargo Ships*, Mitchell and Sawyer's *Empire Ships of World War II*, William H. Miller's excellent new book *First Class Cargo* (2016), and numerous ship-list, ship-spotting and shipbuilding websites.

Company photographs and postcards are acknowledged. Likewise is the valuable contribution made by Harold Jordan. Even so, there are some cards and pictures where I am unsure or unaware of the original source. I hope no offence has been caused, but if some source has not been correctly acknowledged, then I sincerely apologise.

A book touches many people. There have been those locally who have helped in the practical aspects of preparation, including my long-suffering wife, who has put up with me being locked away in the study while putting the manuscript together, and has listened patiently to interesting (?) snippets and progress reports. She used her skill and expertise to check the manuscript for glaring errors of grammar.

Finally, thanks to the excellent team at Amberley, led by the ever gracious and tolerant Connor Stait, for all their help, encouragement and understanding of my inadequate appreciation of the publishing industry in the twenty-first century.

American President Lines, USA

American President Lines was formed in 1938 when the US government took over the assets of the financially defunct Dollar Steamship Company. This could trace its origins back to nineteenth-century lumber shipping by schooner from the Pacific North West. The company had entered trans-Pacific shipping in 1902 and following rapid growth had acquired its first 'President' named ship in 1923. The company encountered serious financial difficulties following the Wall Street Crash in 1929.

In the post-war era, the company continued to operate both passenger liners and passenger cargo liners. Early moves were made into containerisation in 1958. Passenger services declined and eventually ceased in 1973. The company continued as a major container shipper until it was bought by Neptune Orient Line in 1997, before eventually becoming part of the French CMA CGM in 2016.

President Monroe, 1940, 9,500 tons
Built at Newport News, she entered service after the end of the Second World War. A passenger/cargo liner, she housed ninety-six passengers in a very high standard of accommodation, which included separate bathrooms and limited air conditioning. The ships were described as one's American hotel abroad. She was sold to Greece in 1965 to become a pilgrim carrier and was scrapped in Hong Kong in 1969.

President Hoover (ex-*Panama*), 1939, 10,021 tons
Built by Bethlehem Steel, Quincy (MA), she was bought by American President Lines in 1957. She operated, along with her larger running mates, a trans-Pacific service from San Francisco to Honolulu, Yokohama, Hong Kong and Manila. Sold to the Greek Chandris Line in 1964 to become the *Regina*, she was renamed *Regina Prima* in 1967. Laid up in 1976, she was eventually scrapped at Aliaga in 1985. (Postcards courtesy of American President Lines)

Anchor Line

Founded in Glasgow by two brothers in 1838, the brothers initially chartered ships to trade with the Baltic states and Russia. The name Anchor Line first appeared in 1852 and the first ship was acquired in 1854. A new mail, cargo and passenger service was inaugurated from Glasgow to New York in 1856. The company also expanded into the India and Far East trade and it was one of their ships that was the first British ship to steam southbound through the Suez Canal.

In 1911 the company became closely associated with Cunard, but this association ended in 1935. A joint venture was established with the Donaldson Line in 1916 to serve the Glasgow–Canada route.

The company almost collapsed in 1935 but was rescued by the Runciman empire.

The company suffered badly during the Second World War, losing 60 per cent of its fleet.

In the post-war era, changing markets caused the company to struggle. A new joint service to New York was started with Cunard, but by the mid-1960s the company was down to just two ships. The company finally ceased operations in 1980.

Caledonia, 1948, 11,252 tons
Little is known about this ship other than that she was sold to the Netherlands in 1965 to become a floating hotel or hostel, depending on which website you explore.

Sidonia, 1961, 5,705 tons Transferred to the associated Moor Line in 1967 and sold in 1968 to the China Navigation Line to become the *Hupeh*, in 1976 she was converted to be a partial container ship, increasing her overall length by 18 metres. She was sold in 1981 to become the *Sun Opal*, and then the *New United* in 1982, before being scrapped at Kaohsiung in 1985. (Postcards courtesy of Anchor Line)

Naviera Aznar (Aznar Line), Spain

Begun as a partnership in 1902, it became a company – Sota y Aznar – in Bilbao in 1906. The company was split in 1939, becoming Naviera Aznar SA, with liner routes to South America, the Caribbean and the USA. New services were begun from the Canaries to London in 1952, and to Liverpool in 1959, with some cruise activity as well in the 1960s. The company ceased trading in the 1980s.

Monte Urquiola, 1949, 8,392 tons
Built in Bilbao, she was one of six Monasterio class passenger/cargo ships ordered by the Spanish government. Launched as the *Guadalupe*, she was allocated to Aznar Line as the *Monte Urquiola*. Sold to Singapore buyers to become the *Climax Garnet*, she was broken up at Gadani Beach in 1977. (Postcard courtesy of Naviera Aznar SA)

Ben Line (Wm Thomson & Co.)

The original company dated from 1839, when it was W&A Thomson. The company became involved in trading to the Far East in 1859. It took the name Ben Line Steamers in 1919.

In 1966 the company combined with other operators to form Associated Container Transport, providing a container service from European ports to the Far East, Australia and New Zealand.

Although it acquired Sheaf Shipping of Newcastle in 1976, and combined with the Danish East Asiatic Line to operate a weekly service to the Far East in 1991, assets and the remaining ship were sold in 1992.

Benalbanach, 1967, 13,385 tons (dwt) Built by Charles Connell, Glasgow, she was the third of three fast (21 knots) sister ships. After a very brief career with Ben Line, she was sold in 1972 to Italia Line to become the *De Varrazano*. In 1978 she became the Panamanian *Rea B* and the *Razorbill* in 1985, before being broken up at Alang in 1988.

Bendoran, 1956, 12,010 tons Built by Charles Connell, she had the dubious reputation of being the first company ship to cost over £1 million. She was scrapped at Kaohsiung in 1977.

Benloyal, 1959,
10,926 tons
One of three sisters
built by Charles
Connell, marking the
introduction of the
20-knot liner service
on the Far East run.
Initially equipped to
accommodate twelve
passengers, she was
downgraded to
secondary duties in
1972 and was broken
up at Busan, South
Korea, in 1978.

Benlomond, 1957,
10,325 tons
The third of three
large and fast
(17.5 knots) sisters
built by Charles
Connell, Glasgow,
she remained with
Ben Line all her
working life and
was scrapped at
Kaohsiung in 1977.

Benvrackie, 1955,
10,302 tons
The first of the
three sisters built
by Charles Connell,
she had the dubious
distinction of
being the first
to be scrapped
at Kaohsiung in
1975. For once,
I managed to get
a full set of sisters.
(Pictures courtesy of
Ben Line)

Blue Funnel Line

Alfred Holt's Blue Funnel Line was founded in Liverpool in 1865. They traded from Glasgow, Liverpool and Swansea to China, Japan, the Malay Peninsula and the Dutch East Indies. Services to Australia began in 1889 and, in order to compete against the Dutch companies on the east coast of Sumatra, a Dutch subsidiary – Nederlandsche Stoomvaart Maatschappij 'Oceaan' (NSMO) – was established in 1891.

In the early 1960s, Blue Funnel was a substantial player in the liner cargo trade, with the fleet consisting of over seventy ships amounting to over 470,000 gross tons. This total excludes the Glen Line and the Elder Dempster Line fleets, which were also part of the Holt empire. The onset of the container revolution meant that most of the fleet was sold or scrapped during the 1970s, though a few of the ships survived into the 1980s.

S.S. "TYNDAREUS"
KAPAL HAJI SEROMBONG BIRU

Tyndareus, 1916, 11,347 tons

When asking shipping companies for photographs of their ships, size was one of the criteria. That Blue Funnel were still operating a vessel that dated from 1916 was too good to miss, and I was fortunate to get this picture in what must have been the last months of the *Tyndareus'* working life.

Built by Scotts of Greenock, she entered service as a troopship, surviving being mined off Cape Agulhas in February 1917. She eventually entered commercial service in 1920. During the Second World War she served again as a troopship and also as a supply vessel. Returning to peacetime service after the war, she was broken up in Hong Kong in 1960.

Talthybius (ex-*Polydorus*, ex-*Salina Victory*), 1944, 7,671 tons
Blue Funnel sustained heavy losses to its fleet during the Second World War, necessitating the rapid acquisition of war-built standard tonnage at the end of the war. This was a mix of modified Empire ships as well as American-built Liberty and Victory ships.

The *Talthybius* had been built in California as the *Salina Victory*. Bought in 1946, she was initially allocated to Blue Funnel's NSM Oceaan subsidiary as the *Polydorus*. Transferred to the Ocean Steam Company in 1960, she remained in service until she was scrapped at Taipei in Taiwan in December 1971.

On a warm July afternoon in 1965 she is seen steaming 'doon the watter' and approaching Dumbarton.

Perseus, 1950, 10,109 tons
One of four 'P' class ships, she was built by Vickers Armstrong in Newcastle. She was never sold for further trading, but was sold for breaking up in Kaohsiung in January 1973.

Jason, 1950, 10,102 tons
The Helenus class were a quartet of ships operated between the UK, the Far East and Australia. They had accommodation for thirty-six first-class passengers. A victim of the changing trends in travel, she and her sisters were downgraded to twelve passengers in 1965.

Built by Swan Hunter at Wallsend, she had the distinction of being the largest ship in the Blue Funnel fleet. She was also the last ship to operate on Blue Funnel's Australian service.

All the Perseus and Helenus class ships were sold for scrapping in the early 1970s. The *Jason* was scrapped in Kaohsiung in 1972. (Postcards courtesy of Blue Funnel Line)

Centaur, 1964, 8,262 tons
Built by John Brown's at Clydebank, she replaced two smaller pre-war-built ships on the Fremantle–Singapore service. She was a popular ship with accommodation for 190 first-class passengers.

She was also specially equipped to carry sheep and cattle from the Australian ports; although she carried 73,200 passengers during her working life, she also carried 1.1 million sheep! Another unusual feature was the ability to sit on the bottom in ports such as Broome and Derby, where there were high tidal ranges.

By the 1980s the passenger traffic had become uneconomic and the animal trade had gone to specialist animal carriers. She spent two years from 1982 to 1984 on charter, servicing Ascension Island and St Helena.

She was sold to Chinese interests in 1985 and was scrapped in China in 1995.

Achilles, 1957, 7,974 tons

Achilles was one of the many Anchises class ships built for Blue Funnel during the decade following the Second World War. Built by Vickers Armstrong and allocated to the Ocean Steam Ship operating company, she was renamed *Dardanus* in 1972, before being sold to Maçao buyers in 1973. Following a further change of ownership and flag in 1977, she was broken up in Calcutta in 1982. This is one of my own shots, which was taken on a warm summer's day in Glasgow in 1969.

Prometheus, 1967, 12,094 tons

One of eight fast (21 knots) ships built for both Blue Funnel and Glen Line, the *Prometheus* was built by Vickers Armstrong at Newcastle. Sold to C. Y. Tung in 1979, after several internal transfers she was sold for scrap and broken up at Kaohsuing in 1986.

Blue Star Line

Blue Star Line owed its origins to the enterprising Liverpool-based Vestey brothers, who were importing frozen meat from South America. The high shipping charges prompted the operation of their own ships from 1911. After the First World War, the famous 'Star' names appeared and, as operations expanded, the company was regarded as serious competition to the Royal Mail Group.

In the post-war era the company developed global interests and, in the move towards containerisation, became a founding partner of Associated Container Transport. Blue Star was bought by P&O Nedlloyd in 1998 and the last true Blue Star liner was broken up in 2003.

Blue Star Line contributed to my collection, but I have special family reasons for including some of my own pictures in this section.

Colorado Star (ex-Raeburn), 1952, 8,292 tons
Built by Harland & Wolff for the Liverpool-based Lamport & Holt Line, she was transferred to Blue Star Line in 1958. In 1972 she was transferred to the Austasia Line as the *Mahsuri* and returned to Lamport & Holt as the *Roland* in 1977. She was scrapped at Faslane in 1978.

On a warm July afternoon in 1969, she is seen moving 'doon the watter' from Glasgow and passing the impressive hammerhead crane that still stands as a tribute to Glasgow's industrial and shipbuilding heritage.

Paraguay Star, 1948, 10,722 tons
She was one of a quartet of large, virtually identical refrigerated passenger cargo liners that were built by Cammell Laird at Birkenhead. They had accommodation for fifty-three passengers and operated on the UK–South America run, and were thus appropriately named.

Sadly, she came to an ignominious end, catching fire while unloading in the Royal Docks in August 1969. Declared a constructive total loss, she was towed to Hamburg for scrapping. (Photograph courtesy of Blue Star Line)

Fremantle Star, 1960, 8,403 tons
Blue Star Line ships were always among some of the most elegant and stylish of ships. Built by Cammell Laird at Birkenhead, she served briefly with Lamport & Holt Line in 1965. She was sold in 1979 to become the *Catarina* under the Singaporean flag, but was then broken up the same year in Kaohsiung.

This is one of my own pictures, which was taken in London's Royal Albert Dock in February 1966. The date suggests that it was one of my first attempts at colour photography.

Ulster Star, 1959,
10,413 tons
A refrigerated cargo liner
with accommodation for
six passengers, she was
built by Harland & Wolff.
She was broken up at
Kaohsiung in 1979.
  This is one of my
own photographs, taken
in Glasgow docks in
July 1965.

Booker Line

Booker Line can trace its origins back to enterprising sugar planters in Demerara. The shipping business was established to bring sugar to Liverpool. From 1900 the business developed away from colonial plantation activities into insurance, distribution and publishing – hence the Booker Prize. The shipping services continued until the 1980s, when Booker withdrew from shipping.

Amakura, 1949, 2,961 tons
Built by Smith's Dock in Middlesbrough, she was sold to Hong Kong buyers to become the *Greenford.* (Photograph courtesy of Booker Line)

Booth Line

Booth Line was founded in Liverpool in 1863, originally to transport light leather to the USA during the Civil War. In 1866 a regular service began from Liverpool to Brazil and the Amazon River. It was the custom from the very beginning to name the ships after saints. The company diversified into civil engineering in 1919, and in 1946 the steamship interests were sold to the Vestey Group, but separate identities were retained.

Anselm (ex-*Thysville*, ex-*Boudouinville*), 1950, 10,854 tons
Built by Cockerill at Hobokon in Belgium, she was renamed in 1957. She was bought by Booth Line in 1961, but transferred to Blue Star Line to become the *Iberia Star*. In October 1965 she became the *Australasia* and was re-registered in Singapore in 1970. She was scrapped in Taiwan in 1973. (Photograph courtesy of Booth Line)

Bowater Steamship Company

The company was established in 1955 to ship newsprint products from both the Baltic and Eastern Canada. The ships had specially adapted holds to minimise the risk of damage to the rolls of newsprint. To navigate the winter conditions of Canada's eastern seaboard, they were also ice strengthened.

Sarah Bowater, 1955,
8,190 tons (dwt)
One of a pair of sisters built
by Denny's of Dumbarton, she
was sold in 1968 and again in
1970, finally being broken up
at Kaohsiung in 1971.

Gladys Bowater, 1959,
6,471 tons
One of the larger ships built
by Denny's of Dumbarton, she
was sold in 1972 to become
the Liberian *Gigi* and again in
1976 to become the *Aginor*.
In 1977 she became the
Greek-owned *Alexandra*. During
1977 she suffered a major
fire off North Africa and was
abandoned. However, the fire
was extinguished and the ship
repaired and returned to service.
    Following sale to Honduras
in 1985, she was scrapped the
same year at Gadani Beach.

Nicolas Bowater, 1958,
7,136 tons
The largest of the Bowater
fleet, she was built by
William Denny, Dumbarton.
Sold in 1973 to become
the Liberian-flagged *Vall
Comet*, she was scrapped
at Gadani Beach in 1977.
(Postcards courtesy of Bowater
Steamship)

Brocklebank Line

Brocklebank Line originally dated from 1801 as a coastal trader operating out of Whitehaven. It expanded into the Indian trade in 1813 following the cessation of the East India Company monopoly. Later treaties in the mid-nineteenth century enabled the company to expand operations into China. Liverpool became the terminal port in 1819. Curiously, the company did not acquire its first steamship until 1889.

The Cunard interest dated from 1911, when shares were acquired. Cunard-Brocklebank was eventually formed in 1968 with a pooling of all cargo ships, and some Cunarders even gained traditional Brocklebank Indian 'Ma' names. However, containerisation and financial losses meant that the company had ceased to exist by 1983.

Brocklebank Line did not contribute any pictures to the collection.

Manipur, 1945, 8,569 tons
Built to replace an earlier ship of the same name that was lost during the Second World War, she was scrapped as part of the Cunard-Brocklebank rationalisation in 1967. She was captured in Glasgow in July 1965.

Markhor, 1963, 6,867 tons
Built by Alexander Stephen, she was one of the first Brocklebank ships to have three-quarters aft superstructure and engines controlled from the bridge. She was sold to Eggar Forrester in 1976, but was chartered back. In her later life she acquired a white hull. After periods of being laid up in the River Fal, she was eventually sold in 1981 to become the Panamanian *Kara Unicorn* and was broken up in Dalien, north-east China, in 1984. One of my own pictures, this was taken in London's Royal Albert Dock.

Buries Markes Limited

Originally a ship management company, it started operating its own ships in the 1930s. By the mid-1960s it had built up a fleet of modern ships amounting to over 120,000 gross tons. The company moved away from tramp steamers to bulk carriers and withdrew from shipping in the 1980s.

La Sierra, 1960
Built by Chantiers de la Méditerranée at La Seyne, she was sold in 1963 to become the *Bacho Kiro*. She was damaged by fire in November 1978 and was broken up at Aliaga in August 1980.

La Falda, 1958, 8,525 tons
Built by Bartrams, she was sold in 1964 to become the *Rupsa*. She was sold again in 1978 to become the *Caron P E* and again in 1980 to become the *Maldive Image*. In July 1982 she was wrecked 50 nautical miles south-west of Mukalla in the Yemen, almost at the end of a voyage with a cargo of rice from Bangkok. (Photographs courtesy of Buries Markes Limited)

Canadian Pacific Steamships Limited

This was a large Canadian shipping company established in the nineteenth century. From 1880 until after the Second World War it was Canada's largest operator on the Atlantic and Pacific oceans.

The ships were always British flagged, largely British manned and not part of Canada's Merchant Marine.

In the 1960s the group moved into container shipping and CP Ships became a totally separate entity in 2001. It is now part of TUI AG's HAPAG-Lloyd division.

Beaverfir, 1961, 4,539 tons
Built by Sarpsberg, Oslo, Norway, she was acquired while being built. She had the distinction of being the first Canadian Pacific deep-sea ship to reach the Great Lakes.

She was sold in 1972 to become the Liberian *Arion*, then again in 1975 to a Venezuelan buyer and again to Grand Cayman interests in 1981. Sadly, she was blown ashore in a storm off Acajutla, El Salvador, in 1982, grounding her on the Barra de Santiago. Sixteen of the twenty-six crew members were lost in this tragedy.

Beaverford (ex-*Empire Kitchener*), 1944, 9,881 tons
One of the twelve large Empire Chieftain class standard fast (15–16 knots) cargo liners, she was built by Robb Caledon of Dundee. She was sold to Hong Kong buyers to become the *Hulda* in 1962.

Beaverglen, 1946,
9,824 tons
An unusual turbo-electric
ship built by Lithgows
of Port Glasgow, she was
sold in 1963 to become
the *Bermuda Hibiscus* and
again in 1965 to become the
Panamanian *Ping An*. On
24 November 1965 she ran
aground some 5 miles from
the Hoek van Holland. Badly
damaged, her remains were
refloated and she was broken
up in the Netherlands.
(Photographs courtesy of
Canadian Pacific)

Clan Line

Clan Line was founded in Liverpool in 1877 by Charles Cayzer and operated passenger service between the UK and India via the Suez Canal. The company became Cayzer, Irvine & Co. in 1879, then the Clan Line Association of Steamers in 1881, based in Glasgow, before becoming the Clan Line of Steamers in 1890.

In 1894 the company expanded operations into the Persian Gulf and North America and began to carry cargo.

The original Cayzer family retained overall control of the company, which, by the 1930s, had become the largest cargo carrying concern in the world.

In 1956 Clan Line was merged with Union-Castle to form British & Commonwealth Shipping Ltd. In the 1970s the enlarged group moved away from shipping into financial services. Clan Line effectively ceased to exist in 1981.

Clan Line were generous contributors to the collection.

Ayrshire, 1956, 9,360 tons
Built by Greenock
Dockyard, she was
regarded as the flagship
of the fleet. Transferred
internally in 1960 to
the Scottish Shire Line
subsidiary, she was wrecked
in 1965 on Socotra
Island in the Arabian
Sea, south-east of Aden.
She was en route from
Liverpool to Australia with
seven passengers and cargo.

Clan Maciver, 1958, 7,413 tons
One of three sisters built by Greenock Dockyard, she was the first British cargo liner with a three-quarters aft superstructure layout. She was sold to Panama in 1979 and was scrapped in Shanghai in 1980.

Clan Malcolm, 1957, 7,554 tons
Built by Greenock Dockyard, after an uneventful life she was sold to Panama in 1979 to become the *Trinity Fair.*

Clan Sutherland, 1951, 8,418 tons
One of seven ships built by Greenock Dockyard for Clan Line and the Pacific Steam Navigation Co., she managed to survive the many changes experienced by her sisters, remaining with Clan Lane until she was scrapped in Hsinkiang in 1971.

Clan Macinnes, 1952, 6,517 tons
Built by Greenock Dockyard, she survived to be sold in 1978 to Kuwaiti buyers, becoming the *Athoub*. She was scrapped at Kaohsiung in 1979.

Clan Matheson, 1957, 7,553 tons
Built by Greenock Dockyard for the Australian service, she had accommodation for twelve passengers. She survived the many changes to be scrapped at Kaohsiung in 1978. (Photographs courtesy of Clan Line)

Robert Colombier, France

Gustav C (ex-*Bethune*), 1948, 3,500 tons

This book is about tramp ships and this is a classic. Despite an antiquated appearance, this ship was built as the *Bethune* by Ateliers et Chantiers de la Loire in 1948 for Soc. Maritime Nationale. Apparent antiquity is also indicated by a counter stern, and below decks she had triple-expansion steam reciprocating engines.

She and many similar ships were used to ship Welsh coal to France, mostly for use by the French railways. Robert Colombier of Bordeaux acquired and renamed her in 1961. She was broken up in Bilbao in 1968.

A classic South Wales port picture, she was captured loading at the hoist in Swansea's Prince of Wales dock in the mid-1960s.

Cia Transatlántica Española (CTE), Spain

CTE was registered as a joint stock company in 1881 and owned thirty-three vessels by 1894. Twenty-one of the ships were used as military auxiliaries in the Spanish-American War of 1898.

Following the First World War there was considerable expansion and modernisation of the fleet. However, much of the fleet was either destroyed or severely damaged during the Spanish Civil War.

Post-1945 recovery was short-lived due to the rise of airline competition and the moving of cargo to more efficient container ships. Between 1960 and 1974 the fleet was sold. Although operations have ceased, the company still exists as a legal entity.

Guadalupe (ex-*Monastro de la Guadalupe*), 1953, 10,226 tons
One of two sister ships bought while being fitted out for another owner, they were redesigned and converted to become passenger/cargo liners with accommodation for 349 passengers (105 first-class/244 tourist) and some 6,000 tons of general cargo. Both ships entered service on the Spain/Portugal to New York and Havana run.

Profitability waned dramatically in the 1960s, and having failed to clinch a deal on a sale to India, the *Guadalupe* was scrapped in 1973.

Montserrat (ex-*Castel Verde*, ex-*Wooster Victory*), 1945, 9,008 tons
Built by the Californian Shipbuilding Corporation as part of the Victory ship programme, she was sold to the Italian Sitmar Line. Bought by CTE in 1957, she was converted into a passenger ship, being scrapped in Spain in 1973. (Postcards courtesy of Cia Transatlántica Española)

Container Ships

If one defines a container ship as a cargo liner capable of turning round in port very quickly, then container ships fit our definition. By the end of the 1960s, they were starting to appear.

Overseas Container Lines (OCL)

OCL was formed in the late 1960s as a joint venture consortium of British & Commonwealth (Clan Line and Union-Castle), Furness Withy, P&O and Blue Funnel. Over the years P&O gradually took control, finally gaining complete control in 1986 with the company becoming P&O Containers. In 1996 it merged with Nedlloyd to form P&O Nedlloyd, which became part of the Maersk Group in 2005.

Atlantic Container Lines (ACL)

ACL was formed in 1965 by a consortium made up of the Swedish Wallenius Lines, Swedish America Line, Rederei A/B Transatlantic and Holland America Line (NASM) to provide a container service across the North Atlantic. They were joined by Cunard and the French CGT in 1967.

Atlantic Span, 1967, 11,995 tons, Sweden Built by Rheinstahl Nordseewerke, in Emden, she was owned by Rederei Transatlantic, hence the Goteburg registry. A notable additional feature was the roll-on/roll-off (RORO) facility, enabling containers to be loaded by being driven straight onboard. Renamed *Atlantic Service* in 1984, she was broken up in Kaohsiung in 1987. ACL is now part of the Italian Grimaldi Group. (Photograph courtesy of ACL)

Jervis Bay, 1970, 26,876 tons
Built by Upper Clyde Shipbuilders and delivered very late as a result of the problems in the British shipbuilding industry at the time, she was never a lucky ship, becoming a victim of the rapidly increasing size of container ships in the 1980s. In 1984, while being towed to the breakers, she was stranded on a breakwater in Bilbao Outer Harbour, having dragged her anchor in heavy weather, and broke in two. She was scrapped in situ.

She is seen in a handheld evening shot in Tilbury, in 1970, when she was brand new.

Cunard Line

Cunard Line did not contribute to the collection but one ship in the fleet was fascinating and is worthy of inclusion.

Andria (ex-*Silverbriar*), 1948, 7,228 tons
Built by J. L. Thompson of Sunderland for the Silver Line around-the-world service, she had accommodation for twelve passengers. The forward funnel was a dummy, housing the captain's cabin, the radio and the chart rooms.

She was bought by Cunard in 1952 for the London–Havre–New York service. The passenger accommodation and public rooms were given over to the officers.

Sold again in 1963 to China Union Line, she became the *Union Faith*. She was totally destroyed by fire following a collision with oil barges off New Orleans in 1969.

J&J Denholm (Scottish Ore Carriers Limited)

James Denholm set up a shipping agency in Greenock in 1866. A feature of the business was joint owning ventures with the many local shipyards. The company diversified away from shipping in the early 1970s.

However, one significant joint venture was Scottish Ore Carriers Ltd, which was established with shipbuilders Lithgows of Port Glasgow.

Ormsary, 1953, 6,859 tons

She was one of a large number of specialist tramp steamers that were designed to supply the UK steel industry with imported iron ore. Unlike traditional tramps, they were on long-term charter to the steel industry, operating a virtual liner service bringing ore to the mills. Built by Lithgows, she was only 427 feet long to enable her to enter the confined facilities at Port Talbot and Irlam.

Photographed entering the Afan estuary at Port Talbot, the *Ormsary,* rendered obsolete by the new facilities at Port Talbot, was eventually scrapped at Bilbao in 1969.

Donaldson Line

The Donaldson Line started in 1855, initially trading from the Clyde to South America. Services to Canada were added in 1880. In 1924 a new service was started from the Clyde to the west coast of North America. This continued until the company was sold to Blue Star Line in 1954. A limited passenger service was operated from the Clyde to Canada during the post-war era. The company was wound up in 1967.

Laurentia (ex-Medina Victory), 1945, 8,349 tons
Acquired and fitted out to operate the Glasgow–Canada service, she had berths for fifty-five first-class passengers. Downgraded to a freighter in 1966, she was scrapped in Kaohsiung in 1967.

Cortona, 1947, 8,289 tons
Cortona was a refrigerated ship built by Hawthorn Leslie at Hebburn on the Tyne. She was sold in 1967 to Greek buyers to become the *Karos* and survived until she was broken up in Kaohsiung in 1980.

Letitia, 1961, 4,667 tons
The smallest member of the post-war fleet was built by Hall Russell in Aberdeen. Sold in 1967 to J&J Denholm to become the *Bibi*, she acquired Liberian registry in 1975 before being sold in 1977 to Mexican buyers to become the *Tepic*. In March 1985, as the Liberian-flagged *Tepora*, she caught fire in the Gulf of Mexico and sank while under tow 450 miles south of New Orleans. (Photographs courtesy of Donaldson Line)

East Asiatic Company (Det Ostasiatiske Kompagni A/S), Denmark

The Danish East Asiatic Company was founded by Hans Neils Andersen in Copenhagen in 1897. The initial objective was passenger and freight services between Denmark, Thailand and what was then the Malay States, the Straits Settlements and the Far East. Eventually, the route network embraced the Indian subcontinent, Indonesia, Australia and New Zealand, as well as the Caribbean and the west coast of North America.

The company was at the forefront in the development and operation of large motor ships with the pioneering *Selandia* being delivered from Burmeister & Wain amid much royal pomp and publicity in 1912. In an era when the number of funnels was an indication of power, the *Selandia* and many of her contemporaries were built without conventional funnels.

The company still exists, retaining considerable interests in Thailand, but as a widely diversified conglomerate.

Jutlandia, 1934, 8,542 tons

This ship represents an interesting combination of styles. She had a maierform bow coupled to a counter stern and four masts reminiscent of the best of Edwardian elegance. The third mast was the exhaust pipe.

Built at the Nakskov yard in Denmark, she has been described as the largest and finest of the inter-war Danish motor liners. She had accommodation for sixty-nine first-class passengers. She operated from a wide variety of European ports to ports around the Malay Peninsula, Singapore, Thailand and Indo-China.

In dry dock when Denmark was invaded by Germany, she was not seized but rather laid up for the duration.

As part of Denmark's contribution to the Korean War, *Jutlandia* was fitted out as a modern hospital ship with theatres and 356 beds. She started service in Pusan, about 200 km from the front line, in March 1951. She eventually did three tours of duty. On the third tour she was equipped with a helicopter pad and was stationed at Inchon, some 40 km from the front line, as a floating MASH unit. During her 999 days of service, 4,981 wounded Allied personnel and well over 6,000 Korean civilians were treated. Only 29 patients died.

In 1960 she became a Royal Yacht and was placed at the disposal of the King of Thailand during an official visit to Scandinavia. Later, in 1963, she again acted as a Royal Yacht to take Crown Princess Margarethe on an official visit to Southeast Asia.

Having completed her final voyage from Bangkok in December 1964, she sailed in January 1965 to Bilbao for scrapping.

There is a memorial of Korean granite in Copenhagen, commemorating her Korean War service.

Kambodia (ex-*Brandenburg*), 1947, 10,461 tons
Originally, she was ordered from Burmeister & Wain by the occupying German government. At the end of the war she was handed over to Denmark as part of war reparations.

Sold in 1969 to the Danish C. Clausen Line to become the *Linda Clausen*, she was scrapped in the early 1970s. (Postcard courtesy of East Asiatic Co.)

Elder Dempster Line

Elder Dempster Line was originally founded in 1868 to trade from Glasgow and Liverpool to West Africa. In 1909 control passed to Sir Owen Philipps' Royal Mail Group. After the collapse of the Royal Mail Group in the 1930s, the company came under the management control of Alfred Holt's Blue Funnel Line. In 1957, when the Nigerian National Line was established, the company took a 33 per cent share, selling out to the Nigerian government in 1961. In 1965 the company came under the complete control of Blue Funnel.

The shipping company ceased when it was sold out to the French Delmas-Vieljeux. The shipping agency was wound up in 2000.

Aureol, 1951, 14,083 tons
The largest ship in the Elder Dempster fleet, she was described as a medium-sized ocean liner. She was built by Alexander Stephen to enable Elder Dempster to operate a fortnightly service from Liverpool to West Africa. She had accommodation for 245 first-class passengers and for a further 100 in cabin class. She was converted to a one-class liner in 1968.

Southampton replaced Liverpool as the UK terminal port in 1972. *Aureol* was laid up in 1974 and was sold in 1975 to become the accommodation ship *Marianna VI* – a role she fulfilled in Saudi Arabia until 1990. Laid up in Piraeus until 2001, she was then towed to Alang for scrapping.

Apapa, 1948, 11,607 tons
Built by Vickers Armstrong at Barrow-in-Furness, she was the third ship to carry the name. Well-appointed with accommodation for first-, second- and third-class passengers, she had been fully air conditioned by 1961. She even carried deck passengers who would travel on short journeys between the various African calling ports. She was sold in 1968 to Hong Kong buyers to become the *Taipooshan*.

Accra, 1947, 11,600 tons
Accra was also built by Vickers Armstrong at Barrow-in-Furness for the Liverpool–West Africa service. Economic and political unrest led to a decline in trade and she was sold for scrapping at Cartagena in 1967.

Elders & Fyffes Line

Elders & Fyffes Line owes its origin to a partnership established in 1888 to grow and import bananas into the United Kingdom from the Canary Islands. In 1901 the firm was merged with Elder Dempster, who had begun importing bananas from Jamaica, to form Elders & Fyffes. The new company began importing bananas in specially constructed ships to ensure that the fruit arrived in Europe in good condition.

The Fyffes company is now a multibillion-euro listed Irish public company and a major player in the fruit production, distribution and marketing industry.

Chirripo, 1957, 6,283 tons
Also built in Glasgow by Alexander Stephens & Sons, she was sold to Honduras in 1969 to become the *Olancho*, and again in 1972 to become the Greek-owned *Mardinia Exporter*. She was broken up in Kaohsiung, Taiwan, in 1974.

Golfito, 1949, 8,687 tons
Built in Glasgow by Alexander Stephen & Son, she was a classic passenger/cargo liner, operating from either Southampton or Avonmouth to Jamaica, Barbados and Trinidad. She had three passenger decks with cabins for ninety-four first-class passengers. In addition there were public rooms and open-air deck spaces. She had four refrigerated holds with a capacity for 1,750 tons of bananas. She was scrapped at Faslane in 1972.

Matina, 1946, 6,801 tons
Elders & Fyffes suffered heavy losses during the Second World War. The *Matina* was the first of the post-war new constructions from Alexander Stephens in Glasgow. After a useful life of twenty-two years, she was scrapped in 1968.

Changuinola, 1957, 6,283 tons
Built by Alexander Stephens, she frequently was seen operating out of Avonmouth. She was transferred to Empresa Hondurena de Vapores S A as the *Omoa* in 1970. She was scrapped at Dalmiur in 1975.

Camito, 1957, 8,502 tons
Although completed by Alexander Stephen some nine years later, she was a near sister to the *Golfito*, having similar cargo and accommodation specifications to the earlier ship. After a short life of only sixteen years, she was scrapped in Taiwan in 1973.

Chicanoa, 1958, 6,430 tons
Elders & Fyffes remained very loyal to Alexander Stephens. Transferred in 1970 to Honduran ownership in 1972 and renamed *Orica*, she was sold on to Greek buyers in 1972 and was scrapped in 1974. (Pictures courtesy of Elders & Fyffes)

Ellerman Line

The Ellerman Line was founded in the nineteenth century and expanded largely by acquisition to become one of the largest shipping companies in the world, trading globally. The 1967 edition of *Ocean Ships* describes the routes as too numerous to give in detail. In the 1960s, the fleet consisted of some fifty-nine ships, all of which were built post-war.

In the late 1960s Ellerman joined the Associated Container Transport Group and started the successful containerisation of its Mediterranean services. There was also close working with the Scottish Ben Line, with a number of ships being transferred between the two fleets. During the 1970s the company diversified its activities. The business was sold in 1983 and the shipping activities eventually became part of Trafalgar House in the form of Cunard-Ellerman. This was sold to the Andrew Weir Group and then on to German Hamburg-Sud in 2003. By 2004 Ellerman had ceased to exist.

Ellerman did contribute to the collection, but some of my own efforts are also included.

City of Chicago, 1950, 7,622 tons
Built by Vickers-Armstrong at High Walker, she was sold to Greek buyers in 1967 to become the
Kaptamarco. In 1970 she was renamed *Marco* and was broken up in Shanghai in 1971.

In April 1966, following an undergraduate prank on the Middlesbrough Transporter Bridge, we
trespassed in the Middlesbrough docks to obtain this photograph.

City of Durban, 1954, 13,345 tons
One of a stylish quartet built by Vickers Armstrong for the UK–South Africa service. She was
capable of carrying 100 passengers in a high degree of style and comfort. They were regarded
as some of the best ships in the trade. Sold when the service was discontinued in 1971, it was
expected she would join her sisters as a car ferry, but she was eventually sold for scrapping in
Taiwan in 1974, being the first of the quartet to be scrapped.

City of Hull, 1947, 8,458 tons
Built by Vickers Armstrong at High Walker, she was sold for scrapping in 1967, taking the name *Essex* for her final voyage to the breakers in Japan.

City of Ottawa, 1950, 7,622 tons
One of the ten-ship Oxford class built in several yards – in this case by Vickers Armstrong at High Walker – as part of the post-war reconstruction programme, she was renamed *City of Leeds* in 1975 and was sold in 1975 to become the *Gulf Venture*. She was broken up at Gadani Beach in 1977. She was photographed on a rare visit to Avonmouth in the spring of 1969.

City of New York, 1947, 8,420 tons
Built by Vickers Armstrong on Tyneside, she was sold in 1967 to become the Greek *Kavo Matapas* and was broken up at Kaohsiung in 1969.

City of Newcastle, 1956, 7,727 tons
Built by Alexander Stephen & Sons, Glasgow, she was chartered to Ben Line from 1968 to 1970 as the *Benratha*. She reverted to her original name in 1970 and was sold in 1978 to Singapore buyers to become the *Eastern Envoy*. She was broken up in Chittagong in 1980.

Federal Line

Federal Line traced its origins back to 1895. From 1904 it operated a joint service with Houlder Bros to Australia and New Zealand. It was taken over by New Zealand Line in 1916 but continued to trade as a separate concern.

Official photographs of Federal Line ships are absent as, since they were regular visitors to both Swansea and London, I probably photographed the whole fleet. Both photographs were taken in the Royal Albert Dock during the mid-1960s.

Somerset, 1962, 7,602 tons
Built on the Clyde and transferred to P&O in 1973 as part of the great reorganisation. She survived long enough to be sold to Greece to become the *Aegean Sky* in 1980.

Suffolk, 1939, 11,145 tons
Built by John Brown on the Clyde, she was the third of three sister ships that were regarded as some of the finest long-distance cargo liners of the day. A refrigerated ship, she had 535,000 cubic feet of refrigerated cargo capacity. She was scrapped in Kaohsiung in 1968.

French Line (Cie Générale Transatlantique (CGT)), France

CGT was founded in 1861. It originally operated from Le Havre to Mexico, but services to New York were added in 1864. There were also services to the Caribbean, the Mediterranean and Canada.

Like Cunard, there was a large fleet of cargo and cargo liners and the fleet was actually larger than that of Cunard, with the company becoming a serious rival with magnificent ships such as the *Ile de France* and fast record breakers like the *Normandie*.

In 1973 the company was merged with Cie Messageries Maritimes to form Cie Générale Maritime (CGM).

CGT always seemed to favour sending official company photographs.

Gouverneur Générale Chanzy, 1921, 4,384 tons
Another one I could not resist because of her age; built in Birkenhead by Cammell Laird (ship No. 877), she was seized by the Italians in 1941 and was transferred to the Germans in 1943. Scuttled in 1944, she was raised and returned to peacetime service in 1946. She was scrapped in 1963.

Michigan, 1959, 9,235 tons
One of four sister ships built by Chantiers et Ateliers de Provence, Port-de-Bouc, for the Euro–Pacific service from Europe to the Pacific coast of North America. This was a joint service operated by CGT, the German HAPAG and the Dutch NASM.

Displaced by container ships, she was sold in 1976 to Singapore buyers to become the *Brani Island*, and was eventually broken up at Gadani Beach in 1980.

Furness Withy Line

Furness Withy came into existence in 1891. Through its own operations, and obtaining both the Prince Line and the Johnson Warren Line, it was a substantial shipping player in the early 1960s. It also acquired Royal Mail Lines in 1965, the Houlder Group in 1968 and Manchester Liners in 1970.

In 1969 it joined with British & Commonwealth, P&O and Blue Funnel to form Overseas Containers Limited. That operation was acquired by C. Y. Tung's Orient Overseas Container Line in 1980.

Pacific Stronghold, 1958, 9,439 tons
Built by Vickers Armstrong at High Walker, Tyneside, she was sold to Greek buyers to become the *Aegis Honour*. Transferred to Cypriot ownership and flag in 1972, she was broken up in 1974. (Courtesy of Harold Jordan)

Glen Line

The Glen Line owed its origins to a Glasgow-based partnership founded in the mid-nineteenth century – hence the 'Glen' names. Taken over by the Royal Mail Group in 1910, it was integrated with the Shire Line, which is why some of the ships were named for Scottish glens while others were names for Welsh shires. The collapse of the Royal Mail Group in 1930 eventually led to Glen Line being acquired and rescued by rival Liverpool-based Alfred Holt's Blue Funnel Line in 1935, becoming the London end of that operation.

Ships were frequently transferred between the two fleets by merely changing the name and funnel colours.

Denbighshire, 1939, 8,983 tons
One of a class of eight fast (17 knots) twin-screw ships ordered from several yards in the late 1930s, the *Denbighshire* was built by Nederlandsche Scheepvaart in Amsterdam and was one of three to be delivered by the outbreak of the Second World War.

She survived the war and remained with Glen Line until she was transferred to Blue Funnel Line as the *Sarpedon* in 1967. I recall seeing her in Swansea with her new name but still sporting the red Glen Line funnel. She was scrapped at Kaohsiung in 1969.

Glenearn, 1938, 9,088 tons
Also one of the eight fast cargo liners built at the end of the 1930s, she was built by Robb Caledon, Dundee, and was requisitioned to be a naval transport, and later an infantry landing ship.

Returned to peacetime service after the war, she continued in service until she was scrapped in 1970. (Postcards courtesy of Glen Line)

Flintshire, 1962, 11,926 tons

The *Flintshire* was one of a batch of four sister ships delivered in 1962. Typical of the newer ships being built at the time, she was some 40 feet longer than other ships in the fleet and was considerably faster, being capable of 20 knots. She and her sisters were the last Blue Funnel/Glen Line ships to have the traditional vertical profile.

Two of the four sisters were built by Fairfields on the Clyde, but the *Flintshire* was built in the Netherlands. She was sold in 1978 and was scrapped in Taiwan in 1979.

This is one of my own pictures, but given their place in cargo liner history it would have been invidious to have omitted one of these elegant sisters.

Radnorshire, 1967, 13,300 tons

A refrigerated ship built by Vickers Armstrong, she was one of the last eight conventional cargo liners that were built for the Blue Funnel group.

In 1973 she was transferred to Blue Funnel as the *Perseus*. In 1978 she was sold to Hong Kong interests to become the *Kwang-Si*, becoming the Panamanian-flagged *Asia Dragon* in 1982 and the Saudi-flagged *Saudi Zam Zam* in 1983. She was broken up in China in 1984 after only seventeen years' service.

Although capable of carrying containers and working as an 'omni ship', she was typical of many 1960s-built ships – fast but out of date from the very start of their working lives.

This is one of my own pictures, which was taken in London's Royal Docks in March 1969.

HAPAG-Lloyd, Germany

The present HAPAG-Lloyd is the world's fifth largest container carrier. It was formed in 1970 from a merger of two famous nineteenth-century German steamship companies: Hamburg America (HAPAG), dating from 1847, and Norddeutscher Lloyd (NDL), dating from 1856. They were essentially Germany's equivalent of Cunard and White Star and their ships were frequent and successful challengers for the Blue Riband.

The pictures are not photographs or postcards, but have been salvaged from desk calendars.

Moselstein, 1954, 6,968 tons
Built by HDW in Hamburg for NDL, she survived the merger. In 1977 she was sold to Panamanian buyers and was eventually scrapped in Calcutta in 1982.

She illustrates an early attempt at containerisation – an 'omni ship', capable of carrying containers and general cargo. She is seen heading down the Firth of Clyde in August 1971.

Ludwigshafen, 1970, 9,645 tons
She was one of the last conventional cargo liners to be built for HAPAG by HDW Hamburg as an 'omni ship', with a container capacity of 425 TEUs. She was lengthened and converted to a full container ship in Bremen in 1978. Eventually acquired by Mediterranean Shipping (MSC) as the MSC *Giulia* in 1993, she survived to be scrapped at Alang in 2009.

Saarland, 1957, 8,299 tons
Built for HAPAG by Deutsche Werft in Hamburg, she survived the merger and was eventually sold in 1977 to become the *Franca*.

Thuringia, 1967, 8,136 tons
A famous name in the HAPAG fleet, she remained with the company until she was sold to Hong Kong buyers in the 1980s.

Harrison Line

The Harrison Line (officially T&J Harrison) was founded by two brothers in Liverpool in 1853. Initially it traded by importing brandy from the Charente area of France. Later it expanded activities to Iberia, India, East Africa and eventually to the West Indies and Central America. The company ceased trading in 2000.

Harrison Line named their ships for trades and professions, although this was widely interpreted.

Film buffs will note that the inspiration for the book and film *Whisky Galore* was centered on the wartime wreck of the Harrison liner *Politician*.

Author, 1958, 8,715 tons
The *Author* was sold in 1978 to Stena Atlantic Line to become the *Humber*.

This is not exactly a postcard, but a piece of advertising literature. On the back was a fleet list including details of new building ships and a list of UK ports that were served and details of routes that were covered.

Plainsman, 1959, 8,630 tons
The *Plainsman* was built by Doxfords in Sunderland and the card alluded to the Charente S S, which was one of the Harrison Line's trading names, recalling the original link with the French brandy trade. She was sold in 1979 to become the *Evlalia* and was scrapped at Aliaga in 1985.

This was a commercial postcard that I bought in the early 1960s.

Diplomat, 1952, 8,200 tons

One of a series of ten broadly similar ships, she was built by Doxfords, was sold in 1972 to become the Cypriot *Antonios* and was scrapped a few years later.

Not all the photographs in this book are official company pictures. The shortfall has allowed me to top up the numbers with a few pictures of my own in various European ports. On a July afternoon in 1965 I captured the *Diplomat* discharging cargo in Greenock.

Henderson Line (British & Burmese S. N. Co.)

Henderson Line originally developed from a Glasgow–Italy service established in 1829. In 1845 a service from Glasgow to Bombay and Australia was started, followed in 1848 by an emigrant service to New Zealand that called in to Burma on the way back. The British & Burmese Company was formed in 1874.

In 1947 the ships were chartered to Elder Dempster Line and were eventually sold out in 1952. The Six-Day War and closure of the Suez Canal brought an end to the Burma services and the last Henderson ships, having spent the remainder of their lives on the West Africa run, were sold in 1970.

Bhamo, 1975, 5,932 tons Built by Lithgows at Port Glasgow, following the demise of the Burmese service she was transferred to the Guinea Gulf Line and was scrapped in Kaohsiung in 1979. (Photograph courtesy of Henderson Line)

Houlder Line

Houlder Bros was formed in London in 1856, initially using chartered tonnage. It acquired its first ship in 1861. The River Plate passenger/cargo service began in 1881.

A joint venture was established in 1914 with Furness Withy to operate a service to Argentina.

Shipping operations ceased in 1987.

Oswestry Grange, 1952, 9,406 tons
Many of the Houlder Line ships carried names ending in 'Grange'. Four ships carried the name *Oswestry Grange*, including the last ship operated by the company.

The third *Oswestry Grange* depicted here was built by Hawthorn Leslie at Hebburn on the Tyne. She was sold to Greek buyers in 1971 and acquired Panamanian registry in 1978. She was broken up at Gadani Beach in 1979. (Photograph courtesy of Houlder Bros)

Irish Shipping Limited, Ireland

Irish Shipping Limited was set up in 1941 as a wartime expediency to enable the neutral Irish Republic to import and export essential goods and services. After a post-war period of growth and success, there were twenty ships in the fleet by 1960. Difficulties in the early 1960s led to some ships being sold and to others being downgraded off their regular routes. Fleet rationalisation was necessary in the early 1960s, but renewed optimism and confidence returned at the end of the decade.

New ships were ordered and commissioned, but a further downtown in the early 1980s sadly resulted in the company being liquidated in November 1984.

Irish Poplar, 1956, 8,012 tons
An extremely stylish ship originally built for the North Atlantic liner trade, she had some refrigerated capacity and was capable of 16 knots. Following the decline in the liner trade she was downgraded to a tramp and chartered. She was sold to Cypriot buyers in 1972.

Irish Spruce, 1957, 8,019 tons
Sister to the *Irish Poplar,* her career followed the same pattern until she ran aground on the Quita Sueño Bank, off the coast of Nicaragua, in 1972. Declared a constructive total loss, she was sold for scrap.

Mitsui Line, Japan

In 1964, a merger took place between Mitsui Line and Osaka Shosen Kaisha to form Mitsiu-OSK Line, which is readily recognised today by its MOL logo emblazoned on the side of the ships' hulls and the crocodile carrying a container.

Awajisan Maru, 1952, 6,746 tons
This freighter survived the merger. The picture was taken on the Thames in 1955.

Nippon Yusen Kaisha (NYK), Japan

Dating from 1885, NYK is one of the oldest and largest shipping companies in the world. For most of the twentieth century it was the dominant Japanese shipping company. The first container ship entered service in 1968.

Sapporo Maru, 1961, 9,328 tons
Built in Nagasaki, she was the last of fifteen fast (18+ knots) 'S' class ships for the Japan–Europe and US services. In 1970 she had her refrigerated capacity increased and was moved onto the east coast of South America route. She was disposed of at the end of the 1970s.

Still in existence, the company owns in excess of 700 ships, including container ships, bulk carriers and car carriers. The container shipping business is to be merged in 2018 with that of KKK (K Line) and Mitsui-OSK Line.

Saikyo Maru, 1961, 9,558 tons
She was one of fifteen fast (17+ knots) 'S' class ships to be built from 1955 to 1961. Seven were built in Yokohama and the remainder in Nagasaki. Displaced by containerisation in the 1970s, she and her sisters were sold to Far Eastern buyers.

Yamagata Maru, 1965, 10,481 tons
She was one of three 'Y' class ships built by Mitsubishi from 1962 to 1965. It was a response to the trend towards fast (20-knot) cargo liners being operated by both European and American shipping companies. They initially maintained a service between Japan and Europe.

She was sold in 1979 to become the *African Express*, flying the Panamanian flag, and was eventually scrapped in China in 1984.

One of my own photographs, she was seen in London's King George V Dock.

Ise Maru, 1965, 9,917 tons
The 'Y' class ships were quickly followed by the similar but slightly slower (18 knots) 'I' class ships. The *Ise Maru* was sold in 1978 to become the Panamanian-flagged *Char An*. The later 'K' class were considered worth converting to full container ships. (Postcards courtesy of NYK Line)

Lloyd Triestino, Italy

Founded as Osterreichischer Lloyd in Austrian Trieste in 1836, the company managed most of the ocean passenger and cargo trade for the Austro-Hungarian Empire. The company became Lloyd Triestino in 1919, when Trieste became part of Italy. Despite the ravages of two world wars, the company grew to be a major shipping operator, with services from Italian ports to India, the Far East and Australasia as well as East and South Africa. In many respects it was the Italian equivalent of P&O and on the Africa runs was a very serious competitor to British India Line, Ellerman Lines and Union Castle.

In 1993 the company entered into a highly successful partnership with the Taiwanese Evergreen Corporation. The company's name was changed to Italia Maritima in 2006.

As an undergraduate, it was my privilege to get to know R. J. 'Dick' Collins – the London passenger manager of Italia/Lloyd Triestino. He was also an associate of C. M. Squarey, who, sadly, I never met. Even so I did have a first-hand impression of how the discerning traveller preferred the more modern-looking, stylish, faster, better-appointed and all air-conditioned Italian ships when travelling to East Africa. Days were saved by going overland to the Italian departure port as well as avoiding the unpleasant rigors of the Bay of Biscay.

The two ships depicted here were two of four sisters built for the Mediterranean–Africa service.

It is a reflection on the quality and popularity of the service that it was the last to cease running, outliving both British and French competition.

Africa, 1952, 11,434 tons
Laid up in 1976, she was
renamed *Protea*, before
being scrapped in 1980.

Europa, 1952, 11,440 tons
Sold in 1976 to Saudi
Arabia, she caught fire and
sank off Jeddah. (Courtesy
of Harold Jordan)

Lykes Lines, USA

Lykes Line traces its origin back to the American Civil War when Dr Howell T. Lykes started collecting and delivering cattle to the Confederate soldiers in Florida. Later, cattle and fruit were also being shipped to Cuba. The company came into being in 1898 and ships were named for family members.

Originally specialising in trade between the US Gulf Coast ports, the Caribbean and South America, expansion into Europe, the Far East and the Mediterranean began in the 1920s. By 1954 it had the rare distinction of being the largest US cargo fleet still in private ownership. Shares were first offered to the public in 1958.

In 1997 Lykes Lines became part of CP Ships and, following a further takeover by the German TUI Group, the brand name disappeared in 2005.

Almeria Lykes, 1945,
7,855 tons
A standard C3-S-BH1
cargo ship built by Federal
Shipbuilding & Dry Dock
at Kearny (NJ), she served
the fleet until she was
scrapped at Kaohsiung
in 1971.

Joseph Lykes, 1960,
9,887 tons
At the turn of the 1960s,
Lykes Lines embarked on a
programme to replace all the
old standard ships. A new,
very distinctive, standard
ship, the C3-S-37a, was
developed. The *Joseph Lykes*
was built by Ingall
Shipbuilding at Pascagoula,
Mississippi. In 1971 she was
converted into a container
ship, was downgraded to
a barge in 1992 and was
scrapped in 1996.

A. P. Møller's Maersk Group, Denmark

A. P. Møller's Maersk Group was first established in 1904 in Svendborg on the island of
Funen in south-central Denmark. It established its own shipyard at Odense after the First
World War. A tanker business was established in 1926 and a liner service to the Far East
via the Pacific in 1928. By 1939 it was the second largest shipping company in Denmark.

During the Second World War, all ships served with the US Navy.

The post-war era saw substantial reconstruction and growth. The last traditional
cargo ships were delivered in 1967 and the first container ship was delivered in 1973. By
1993 the company was the largest container line in the world, and it also operated some
of the largest container ships in the world. Collaboration with P&O Nedlloyd began in
the 1990s, with its complete acquisition taking place in 2005. Also acquired during this
period was the South African Safmarine.

Continued growth and acquisition within the transport and energy sectors has led to
annual revenues in excess of $47 billion.

Charlotte Maersk, 1967, 10,928 tons

One of the seven Cecilie Maersk class built for the Europe–Far East fast (23 knots) service. They were the last traditional cargo liners to be built for the group. In 1981 she was lengthened and broadened by Hitachi Zosen into a fully cellular 1,218 TEU capacity container ship. Sold in 1987 to China Ocean Shipping to become the *Tao He*, she was eventually scrapped at Xingang in 1998.

Maersk Line were never asked to contribute to the collection, and, unlike today, their ships were rare in UK ports in the 1960s. I felt it would be wrong to omit one of the world's largest shipping companies from this collection. (Photographed by M. J. 'Sandbanks' Goodwin in Hamburg in 1968)

Manchester Liners

Manchester Liners was a cargo and passenger shipping company that was formed in 1898 and operated services from the inland port of Manchester across the Atlantic. It was also an associate company of the Furness Group.

The company successfully moved into containerisation in the 1960s, but restrictions imposed by the Manchester Ship Canal meant it could not compete. Operations ceased in 1985.

Manchester Spinner, 1952, 7,815 tons Little is known about this ship. She was the third ship to carry the name and was sold to Greek buyers in 1968 to become the *Estia*.

Manchester Mariner, 1955, 7,850 tons One of a pair of sisters built by Cammell Laird of Birkenhead, she was sold to Greek buyers to become the *Ira* in 1968, becoming the *Panday Ira* in 1975.

Manchester Shipper, 1943, 7,636 tons Built by Blythswood Shipbuilding, Glasgow, she had the honour of carrying Manchester Liners' first container load. She was broken up in Trieste in July 1969.

Manchester City, 1937, 5,600 tons Built by Blytheswood Shipbuilding on the Clyde, she served as a minelayer during the Second World War and was scrapped at Faslane in 1964.

Manchester Regiment, 1947, 7,638 tons Another Blytheswood product, she was sold in 1967 to become the *Azure Coast II* under the Panamanian flag. She was scrapped in 1971.

Photograph courtesy of Manchester Liners.

Cie des Messageries Maritimes (MM), France

Messageries Maritimes was virtually the French equivalent of P&O. The company dated from 1851, taking the name Cie des Messageries Maritimes in 1871. It traded to East Africa, India and the Indian Ocean, the Far East and French Polynesia.

It merged with CGT (the French equivalent of Cunard) in 1977 to form Cie Générale Maritime (CGM). In 1996 the company was privatised and was sold to Cie Maritime d'Affretement (CMA) to form CMA CGM. The CMA CGM containers are a familiar sight on Europe's roads and railways.

CMA CGM are an example of the typically generous European donors of postcards to my collection.

Caledonien, 1952, 12,700 tons
The company built nine superbly appointed passenger/cargo ships for the Far East services during the early 1950s. They were grouped into a pair that were just under 13,000 gross tons, three over 13,500 tons and a group of four at just under 11,000 tons. The *Caledonien* was one of a pair of sisters within that group of nine. She could accommodate seventy first-class passengers, eighty-four tourist and 208 third-class passengers, and operated to Sydney via the French Caribbean territories and French Polynesia. Laid up and then sold in 1971 to Greek buyers, she was used on the Piraeus–Crete–Cyprus run until she was scrapped in 1975.

Cambodge, 1953, 13,520 tons
Built in Dunkerque, she was one of a trio of ships named for the territories of French Indo-China. She was equipped with five cargo holds and accommodation for 347 passengers. Despite changing commercial and political conditions, the *Cambodge* remained on the Far Eastern run until she was retired in 1969 and laid up in Marseille.

Sold to a Greek operator, she was converted to become the cruising liner *Stella Solaris*, operating in the Eastern Mediterranean and latterly on winter cruises in the Caribbean. She was eventually scrapped in 2003.

Ferdinand de Lesseps,
1952, 10,882 tons
One of the group of slightly
smaller passenger/cargo
ships (*paquebot mixte*)
named for French celebrities.
She operated on the East
Africa trade to Mauritius.

Sold to Greek buyers in
1968 to become the *Delphi*,
she was later sold to a
variety of Greek buyers in
1977 and was eventually
scrapped in 2003 – the last
survivor of the quartet.

Anadyr (ex-*Pierre de
Saurel*), 1947, 4,512 tons
Bought from the French
Fabre Line in 1953, she
was sold in 1964 to
become the *Malagasy*.

Euphrate, 1955,
7,030 tons
Built by Chantiers de la
Méditerranée at La Seyne,
she was one of at least
nine company ships
named for Asian rivers.

She was sold in 1973
to Panamanian buyers
to become the *Elsey
Fir* and was sold again
in 1977 to become the
Orient Clipper. She was
eventually scrapped in
1983.

Kouang-Si, 1957, 6,991 tons
This is another opportunity
to include one of my own
photographs in a different
port. The *Kouang-Si* was one
of the ten-ship Godavery class
built by Chantiers Navale de
La Ciotat. All the ships were
sold during the 1970s, with
the *Kouang-Si* being sold for
scrapping in Kaohsiung.
    She is pictured in
Dunkerque in August 1968.

Sindh, 1956, 7,051 tons
One of the ten-ship
Godavery class, she was built
at La Ciotat. Trapped for
eight years in the Suez Canal
after the 1967 Egypt–Israel
War, she was freed in 1975.
She was then sold to Saudi
Arabia and was scrapped in
1976.

Velay, 1961, 7,508 tons
Built at La Ciotat, she was
one of eight 'V' class ships
constructed in two batches
between 1960 and 1965.
She survived the 1977 MM/
CGT merger to form CGM
(Compagnie Générale
Maritimes) and was sold
in 1979 to become the
Panama-flagged *Char Hang*.
    She was photographed
in Hamburg by my college
friend, M. J. 'Sandbanks'
Goodwin, in 1968.

Pasteur, 1966, 17,986 tons

Although I took my own photograph of this ship in Dunkerque in 1967, this official postcard is clearly a better picture.

The largest and last combo liner built for MM, she was intended for the Marseille–Australia service, but instead operated between Northern Europe and the east coast of South America. She had accommodation for 163 first-class passengers in luxurious conditions and 266 tourist-class passengers.

She was sold to the Shipping Corporation of India (SCI) in 1972 to become the *Chidambaram* and was sadly destroyed by fire in the Bay of Bengal in February 1985. Her burnt out hull was towed to Mumbai for scrapping.

Gallieni, 1954, 4,718 tons

Built by Chantiers et Ateliers de Provence at Port de Bouc, she was one of two sisters designed for the Madagascar and Indian Ocean islands service. She also operated to support French interests in Antarctica. Originally she could accommodate twelve passengers in cabins and 350 deck passengers. Due to the nature of her operations, much of her cargo handling was done into barges and lighters over the side, rather than at established quays. In 1957 she was equipped with a helicopter deck.

Sold in 1972 to Panamanian buyers, she was broken up in Bangkok in 1983. (Postcards courtesy of Cie des Messageries Maritimes)

Mauricien, 1963, 6,872 tons
One of ten virtually identical sister ships, *Mauricien* was built by Normed Construction Navales at La Ciotat. She had an uneventful life, being eventually broken up at Kaoshiung in 1978. She was captured at Dunkerque in August 1967.

Moore-McCormack Lines, USA

The company was founded in 1913 by Albert V. Moore and Emmett J. McCormack and started with one ship trading to Brazil. By the early 1960s it operated over thirty ships, with a further eight being acquired from the Robin Line. It operated from the Eastern Seaboard and the Great Lakes to South America, Europe and South Africa.

Having failed to capitalise on early, pioneering investment in container shipping, the company ceased trading when it was bought out by US Lines in 1982.

Mormacargo, 1963, 10,599 tons
One of six Constellation class ships, she was built by Ingalls Shipbuilding at Pascagoula (MS), entering service in 1964. In an era of fast cargo liners, she was capable of 24 knots. Originally built to a C4-S-60a standard design, she was modified to C6-S-60c in Tampa (FL) in 1982. She became the US Lines *American Argo* in 1983, the *Stella Lykes* in 1986 and finally the *Magallanes* in 1989. In 1992 she went into reserve and was eventually scrapped at Brownsville (TX) in 2006. (Photograph courtesy of Moore-McCormack Lines)

Moss Hutchinson Line

Moss Hutchinson Line was formed in 1934 out of the collapse of the Royal Mail Group. It traded to France, Iberia and the Mediterranean. In 1935 it was acquired by General Steam Navigation, which was itself a wholly owned subsidiary of P&O.

The company retained its separate identity, but disappeared in the major P&O restructuring of the early 1970s.

Tabor, 1952, 3,694 tons
Built by Robb Caledon in Dundee, she survived to become part of the P&O General Cargo Division in 1971. In 1975 she was sold to Greek buyers to become the *Katia* and in 1982 was sold again to Maltese buyers to become the *Kate,* before being scrapped at Beypore in Kerala, India, the same year. (Photograph courtesy of Moss Hutchinson Line)

NASM (Holland America Line), Netherlands

NASM was established in 1873 as the Netherlands' equivalent of Cunard. Like Cunard it operated a transatlantic passenger service. Never a Blue Riband contender, and operating much smaller liners, it was still very highly regarded.

In addition to the passenger liners, there was a network of passenger cargo services to both the east and west coast of North America, which were operated by some twenty ships with a total gross tonnage of over 150,000. Now, like Cunard, only the cruising liners remain.

NASM were particularly generous in their response for my request for pictures.

Sommelsdyk, 1939, 9,227 tons
Built by Odense Staalskipsvaerft, she was the third ship to carry the name. Capable of 15.5 knots, due to her speed she was requisitioned as an armed merchant cruiser during the Second World War and served in that role for the duration of the war.

Westerdam, 1946, 12,149 tons
Built by Wilton-Fijenoord, she was scuttled in 1940 while incomplete. Salvaged and commissioned in 1946, she and her sister the *Noordam* carried 148 first-class passengers on the Rotterdam–New York run. She was sold for scrapping in 1964.

Albasserdyk (ex-*Trumpeter*, ex-*Bastian*), 1943, 8,292 tons
Built as the escort carrier USS *Bastian*, she was transferred to the Royal Navy under Lease/Lend and was commissioned as HMS *Trumpeter*. Returned to the United States at the end of the war, she was acquired by NASM in 1948. She was sold in 1966 to Panama to become the *Irene Valmas* and was scrapped in 1971.

Dinteldyk, 1957, 11,366 tons
Built by Wilton-Fijenoord for the North American west coast service, she carried sixty first-class passengers. Unusually for a NASM cargo liner, she had a grey rather than black hull. Grey hulls were usually reserved for only the top link passenger liners.

Sold to C. Y. Tung in 1970 and renamed *Oriental Fantasia*, she was converted into a container ship. She became the *Hong Kong Success* in 1972 and was sold for breaking up in Kaohsiung in late 1978, with scrapping actually commencing in February 1979.

One of my own photographs, this was taken in London's Royal Albert Dock in February 1966.

Andyk (ex-*Groningen*), 1946, 8,380 tons
Built in 1946 by the Sun Shipbuilding & Dry Dock Company as the *Groningen*, she was acquired the same year. She was sold to a Cypriot buyer in 1969 to become the *Aurora*.

Kloosterdyk, 1957, 5,635 tons
She was one of the six 'K' class fast (16 knots) motor ships that were built to replace the Victory ships that had been acquired immediately after the Second World War. Built by J. Smit in Albasserdam, she was one of three of the sisters built in the Netherlands. To carry large and heavy items of cargo, the ship was equipped with a 40 ton heavy-lift derrick on the foremast.

She was sold in 1970 to become the Yugoslav *Breznice* and was sold again in both 1982 and 1983, becoming the *Utila Princess*. She was finally broken up at Brownsville (TX) in 1986.

Schiedyk, 1949, 9,592 tons
She was one of a pair of sisters built by Harland & Wolff for the Java–New York service. Originally driven by steam turbines, she was re-equipped with diesel engines in 1960.

On 8 January 1968, while en route from Seattle to London, she ran aground at Bright Island (Vancouver) and was abandoned by her crew. She sank the following day. (Postcards courtesy of NASM)

New Zealand Line

New Zealand Line was founded by local farmers and traders in Christchurch (NZ) in 1873. They began operating refrigerated ships in 1882. They merged with the UK-based Federal Line in 1912, but separate identities were retained until the early 1960s, by which time it had become part of the vast P&O empire.

Eventually, the remaining cargo liners became part of the P&O General Cargo division in 1973, and acquired the P&O corporate identity.

Haparangi, 1947, 11,281 tons
One of eight large refrigerated ships that formed a major part of the post-war reconstruction programme, she was built by John Brown at Clydebank. She survived to become part of the P&O General Cargo Division, including acquiring the new corporate blue colours. She was scrapped in the Far East in February 1974.

Otaio, 1958, 13,314 tons
Built by John Brown at Clydebank, she was the company's training ship. She had accommodation and facilities to cater for forty deck and thirty engineering cadets. This meant she had slightly less refrigerated space than some of her sisters. In the autumn of 1961, several of us teenagers were entertained on board and were taken around to tempt us into a life at sea.

She acquired the Federal Line identity in 1966 and survived to become part of the P&O General Cargo Division, complete with its garish corporate blue colour scheme. She was sold in 1976 to become Gulf Shipping Lines' training ship *Eastern Academy* and was eventually broken up at Gadani Beach in 1982.

Otaki, 1953, 10,934 tons
Built by John Brown's of Clydebank, she survived to become part of the P&O General Cargo Division. She was sold in 1975 to Cypriot buyers to become the *Mahmout*. While undergoing a refit in Greece she caught fire and was declared a constructive total loss. She was sold in 1979 and was towed to Izmir in Turkey for breaking up.

Ruahine, 1951, 17,851 tons
Built by John Brown's at Clydebank to work with the larger *Rangitane* and *Rangitoto*, she was the last true passenger/cargo ship in the New Zealand Line fleet. She was capable of carrying 200 passengers and had all the facilities, such as various public rooms, a swimming pool and even a children's play area and nursery. In addition she had over 444,000 cubic feet of refrigerated cargo space. She was sold in 1968 to C. Y. Tung to become the *Oriental Rio* and was broken up in Kaohsiung in 1974.

Rangitane, 1949, 21,867 tons
At over 21,000 gross tons she almost fits into the category of a passenger liner. Built by
Vickers Armstrong on the Tyne, she was the first one-class cargo liner to be operated by New
Zealand Line.

In 1965 her mainmast was removed and she was transferred to the Federal Steam Navigation
Line and lost her pale buff funnel in favour of the Federal insignia.

Sold to C. Y. Tung in 1968, she became the cruising liner *Oriental Esmeralda*, flying the Liberian
flag. Operated as such until 1972, when she was laid up in Hong Kong, she was scrapped in
Taiwan in 1976. (Postcards and photographs courtesy of New Zealand Line)

Remuera (ex-*Parthia*), 1948, 13,362 tons
As the *Parthia* she had the unique distinction of being the only Cunarder built by Harland &
Wolff. She and her sister, the *Media*, were the first passenger ships to be delivered to Cunard after
the Second World War. They were also the first to be fitted with stabilisers. Although she could
accommodate 250 passengers, she was essentially a cargo liner.

She was sold in 1961 to New Zealand Line to become the *Remuera*, being extensively refitted
with improved and extended facilities to accommodate 350 passengers.

In 1964 she was transferred to the Eastern & Australian Steamship Company, becoming the
Aramac on the Melbourne–Hong Kong–Japan run. She was sold for scrapping at Kaohsiung in
1969. (Courtesy of Harold Jordan)

Oranje Line, Netherlands

Formed in 1937 as the Maatschappij Zeetransport to bring fruit from the Mediterranean and North Africa. The original fleet was two former Great Lakes steamers owned by the Norwegian firm of Olsen & Ugelstad. The success of the Norwegian venture motivated the Oranje Line to set up a Great Lakes services in 1938.

The name Oranje Line was taken after the war and regular Great Lakes services were established in 1948. Joint Fjell-Oranje Line services were established in 1955. Oranje Line was bought out by Koninklijke Paketvaart-Maatschappij in 1958, and a year later half the equity was taken by Holland America Line (NASM).

By the late 1960s, however, the company was unable to compete and was liquidated in 1970. The Fjell Line still continues to operate.

Prins Willem IV, 1946, 1,535 tons
She was eventually completed for peacetime service in 1946 at Hardinxveld-Giessendam, a small town east of Dordrecht on the Beneden Merwede in South Holland. In 1967 she was sold to Italian buyers to become the *Citta di Beirut*. She was sold twice more in 1973 and was broken up in Italy in 1974.

Prins Johan Willem Friso, 1948, 2,338 tons
Also built in Hardinxveld-Giessendam, she was sold to Greek buyers in 1968 to become the *Notis*, and in 1973 to become the *Vorras*. She was scrapped at Gadani Beach in 1974.

Prins Frederik Hendrik, 1951, 1,588 tons
Built by De Merwede Hardinxveld-Giessendam, she was sold to Italian buyers in 1966 and was renamed *Michele Garofano*. In 1977 she was wrecked in Benghazi and was subsequently broken up. (Photographs courtesy of Fjell-Oranje Line)

P&O

P&O owes its origins to the establishment in 1835 of a regular steamer service from London to Spain and Portugal. As such, it was probably the first true steamship-operated liner service, antedating Samuel Cunard by five years. The famous house flag owes its origin to the blue and white of the Kingdom of Portugal and the red and yellow of Spain. A mail contract serving Iberia was awarded in 1837, which was followed by a further mail contract to Alexandria, Egypt, in 1840. The original company, Peninsular & Oriental Steam Navigation, was incorporated by Royal Charter in 1840. Services were extended to Singapore in 1845 and by connection to Australia in 1852.

The company grew both by growth and acquisition to become a major shipping line, carrying both passengers and cargo from Europe to India, the Far East and Australasia.

In 1969 P&O became part of Overseas Containers Limited, eventually buying out all its partners by 1986. By this time all of its cargo operations had been converted to containerisation. The many subsidiaries, hitherto operating under separate identities, were absorbed into the P&O Group and its corporate identity.

The shipping activities were eventually merged with Nedlloyd and were later acquired by the Maersk Group.

Remnants of the company still exist and ships sporting a dark blue funnel and famous house flag can still be seen regularly along the Thames Estuary.

Although P&O contributed to my collection, I am unsure of the origin of these pictures. The *Cathay* is one of the famous J. Arthur Dixon postcards, which I appear to have bought at some time for 4½d!

Baradine (ex-*Nardana*), 1956, 8,511 tons
Originally one of four 'N' class ships built for the British India Line's East Africa and Australia routes, she was transferred to P&O in 1963. She reverted to her old name when she returned to British India and survived, albeit briefly, to become part of P&O's General Cargo Division. She was sold to Iran in 1973 and was broken up at Gadani Beach in 1976.

Perim, 1945, 9,550 tons
Built by Barclay Curle, she was scrapped in 1967.

Cathay (ex-*Baudouinville*), 1957, 13,351 tons
Purchased along with her sister, the *Chitral*, from Cie Maritime Belge in 1961, she operated a regular passenger and cargo service to the Far East until 1970. Transferred to the Eastern & Australian Line, she then operated between Australia, the Far East and Japan until she was sold to the Chinese, becoming the *Kenghshin*. In 1976 she was acquired by the China Ocean Shipping Company, was renamed *Shanghai* and remained in service, being well maintained and still carrying passengers until 1996.

Strathbora, 1967, 12,539 tons

The 'Super Straths' were P&O's last conventional cargo liners and deserve representation in this survey.

Built by Mitsui, they operated a fast (21 knots) service to the Far East until 1971. She survived to join P&O's General Cargo Division and acquired the new P&O corporate blue livery, operating on the Arabian Gulf–Japan trade until she was sold to Thailand in 1979, becoming the *Benjamas*. She was scrapped at Kaohsiung in 1986.

One of my own shots, she is seen in the King George V Dock, London.

Palm Line

Palm Line was formed from the United Africa Company in 1949. The company traded along the West African coast from Morocco to Angola. To navigate the many creeks, the ships had to be less than 500 feet long and draw no more than 27 feet. To enter the Escravos River in Nigeria, a maximum of 17 feet was permitted over the bar.

The 1980s saw the end of Palm Line. A decline in traffic between Europe and West Africa resulted in the company being sold in 1986.

Ibadan Palm, 1959, 5,658 tons
Built by Swan Hunter & Wigham Richardson at their Neptune Yard, Low Walker, she complied with the local specification by being only 460 feet long.

She was sold to Kuwaiti buyers in 1978, becoming the *Hind*, and then to Hong Kong buyers in 1979, becoming the *Arunkamal*. Following a further change of ownership in 1980 she was broken up at Gadani Beach in 1983. (Photo courtesy of Palm Line)

Port Line

In 1914 the Commonwealth & Dominion Line was formed from four smaller companies, operating twenty-three ships on the Australia and New Zealand run. It was taken over by Cunard in 1916 and took the distinctive Cunard funnel colours after the First World War. The 'Port' prefix began to appear with new ships after the First World War and the company, always known as the Port Line, was officially branded as Port Line Limited in November 1937.

A founder member of Associated Container Transport in January 1966, the last conventional Port Line ships were transferred to Brocklebank Line in 1982.

Port Huon, 1927, 8,021 tons
She was a refrigerated ship built by Swan Hunter at Wallsend as part of the rebuilding programme to replace war losses. She was capable of carrying twelve first-class passengers in a high degree of comfort and luxury, and with a speed of 14 knots she could complete the Melbourne–London run in thirty-four days. She was scrapped in 1961. (Postcard courtesy of Port Line)

Port Campbell (ex-*Clarkspey*), 1960, 9,685 tons
Built by Lithgows, Port Glasgow, she started life as the *Clarkspey*, being owned by H. Clarkson and managed by Denholm. She was chartered to Port Line from 1961 to 1966. She became the *Kings Reach* in 1969, then the *Alderminster* until 1975. She was briefly the Liberian-flagged *Joli* before taking on her final identity as the Greek-flagged *Flora C.* She was scrapped at Chittagong in 1982.

One of my own photographs, she was captured on the south side of Swansea's King's Dock. Judging by the time frame, it was taken using my old box Brownie.

Reardon Smith Line

The company owed its origins to a West Country entrepreneur and successful mariner who set up as a ship owner in Cardiff in 1906. The company prospered and by 1922 there were thirty-nine vessels in the fleet. In 1928 a regular service from the United Kingdom to the west coast of North America was established under the name Reardon Smith Line.

The company moved away from tramping into bulk carriers in the 1960s, selling all of its tramp steamers by 1972. Ship-owning activities ceased in 1985.

Cardiff City, 1962, 10,335 tons
Built by Doxfords of Sunderland, this large tramp steamer was sold in 1965 to become the *Sara Luper* and was sold again to Hong Kong buyers to become first the *Alpac Asia* and later the *Alpac Ocean.* She was scrapped at Kaohsiung in 1986. (Photo courtesy of Reardon Smith Line)

Royal Mail Line/Pacific Steam Navigation Company

The Royal Mail Steam Packet Company was founded in 1839. It grew largely by acquisition to become a major player in ocean shipping until its spectacular collapse in 1932. Royal Mail Lines was salvaged by the government from the collapse and concentrated on liner services from the UK and Iberia to the West Indies and South America. The company was bought by Furness Withy in 1965 and rapidly lost its separate identity.

Pacific Steam Navigation had been founded in London in 1838 and operated services to the Pacific coast of South America. It was the first company to use steam ships in the Pacific Ocean and was taken over by the Royal Mail Group in 1910. Name, routes and a separate identity remained until the company was bought by Furness Withy in 1965.

Durango, 1944, 9,806 tons
She was built by Harland & Wolff under a commercial contract as a refrigerated ship working the North Pacific route. In 1965 she was transferred to Shaw Savill Line as the *Ruthenic* and was scrapped in Taiwan in 1967.

Loch Loyal, 1957, 11,035 tons
Also built by Harland & Wolff for the North Pacific service, she was sold in 1971 to become the *Aegis Loyal* and was scrapped in Shanghai in 1974.

Cuzco, 1951, 8,038 tons
Sold to Ben Line to become the *Benattow,* she was eventually scrapped in 1977.

Salamanca, 1948, 6,204 tons
Another product from the slipways of Harland & Wolff, she was sold to Greek buyers in 1967 to become the *Kronos.*

Pizarro, 1955, 8,564 tons
Following the delivery of two ships originally ordered by Clan Line from Greenock Dockyard, Pacific S. N. ordered two more from the same yard. The *Pizarro* was the second of this pair. She passed to Royal Mail Lines in 1970 and was sold in 1972 to Greek buyers, becoming the *Kavo Maleas*. She was broken up in Kaohsiung in 1974.

Ebro, 1952, 7,784 tons
Built by Harland & Wolff at their Govan yard for the Caribbean and Latin America service, she was sold in 1969 to Hong Kong buyers to become the *Fortune Victory* before being sold on to Burma Five Star Line to become the *Kalewa*. She was broken up in China in 1979. (Pictures courtesy of Royal Mail Lines and Pacific S. N.)

Royal Netherlands Steamship Co. Ltd (KNSM)

Operated services from 1870 from north-west Europe to the Dutch East Indies (Indonesia) via the Suez Canal. Other transpacific routes followed, which were further developed after Indonesian independence.

In 1970 the company merged with United Netherlands (VNSM) and Rotterdam Lloyd (KRL), eventually forming Nedlloyd. In 1996 Nedlloyd merged with P&O and the combined group became part of the Danish Maersk Group in 2005.

Prins der Nederlanden, 1957, 7,552 tons
One of a pair of sisters built for the Europe–Caribbean service, unusually for a cargo liner she carried two classes of passengers: 116 in first class and sixty-eight in economy. Most cargo liners only carried first-class passengers. (Postcard courtesy of KNSM)

Scindia Steam Navigation Company, India

One of the oldest Indian shipping companies, Scindia S. N. Co. was founded in 1919 by entrepreneurs from Gujarat. By the 1960s it had extensive cargo liner services to Europe, East and West Africa, the Pacific coast of North America and the Great Lakes.

A victim of the global slump of the 1980s, trading ceased and the company had withdrawn from all shipping relating activities by 1997.

Jaladurga, 1960, 9,176 tons A refrigerated ship built by Flender Werft in Lübeck, Germany, she remained with the company until she was scrapped in Calcutta in 1985. (Photograph courtesy of Scindia S. N.)

Shaw Savill Line

The Shaw Savill Line dated originally from 1858, trading to Australia and New Zealand. After the First World War, many of its services to Australasia were via the Panama Canal. In 1928 it was bought out by the famous White Star Line.

Following White Star's merger with Cunard, White Star withdrew from the Australia and New Zealand services. Shaw Savill passed into the control of the Furness Withy Group but retained its separate identity and two classic White Star features – the buff funnel with the black top and the names ending in 'ic'. In subsequent years, many White Star names reappeared on Shaw Savill Line ships.

Athenic, 1947, 15,182 tons Described as a refrigerated cargo/passenger ship, she was one of the first peacetime orders placed with Harland & Wolff. She was launched in Belfast on Tuesday 26 November 1946 and was delivered in July 1947. She was scrapped in Taiwan in 1969.

Gothic, 1948, 15,911 tons
Built by Swan Hunter at Wallsend on Tyne, she was completed in December 1948. Her main claim to fame was serving as the Royal Yacht for the Commonwealth Tour from November 1953 until May 1954. Along with the *Corinthic* she operated on a passenger service to New Zealand via the Panama Canal. While on this service between Wellingon and Panama she suffered a major fire in August 1968, in which seven people sadly died. She was delivered for scrapping in Taiwan in August 1969.

Corinthic, 1947, 15,682 tons
Built by Cammell Laird at Birkenhead, she was one of the largest refrigerated ships on the Australia/New Zealand run. She had 510,000 cubic feet of refrigerated cargo space and had accommodation for eighty-five first-class passengers. Downgraded to a cargo-only ship in 1965, she was scrapped at Kaohsiung in 1969.

Ceramic, 1948, 15,896 tons
Also built by Cammell Laird, she remained a passenger/cargo liner for all her working life, which ended in a Belgian scrapyard in 1972. (Postcards courtesy of Shaw Savill Line)

Silver Line

Dating from 1908, by the 1930s the company was offering a round-the-world passenger service for £100!

The company moved into bulk carriers in the mid-1960s, and into tankers and chemical tankers in the 1970s, but ceased to exist in 1985.

Silverbeck, 1960, 9,542 tons
This large tramp steamer was built by Bartram & Sons, Sunderland, and was sold to Yugoslav buyers in 1965 to become the *Durmitor*. Sold again to Greek buyers in 1979, and finally to Sri Lankan buyers, becoming the *Ceylon Sailor* in 1982; she was broken up at Karwar, South India, in 1984. (Photograph courtesy of Silver Line)

South African Marine Corporation (Safmarine), South Africa

Going through my collection of photographs, I discovered that we can trace the progress of a successful shipping company through the turbulent years of transition.

Safmarine owes its origin to a pioneering venture established in 1946 by South African industrialists and American ship owners. Services began following the acquisition of three Victory ships. During the 1950s and 1960s there was a strong association with the UK-based British & Commonwealth shipping group. The company has grown to become a major north/south operator that is noted for its African expertise.

In 1999 the company became part of the Danish Maersk Group but retains much of its individual identity. Safmarine containers can be readily observed on European roads and railways, and the ships retain their grey hulls, with Safmarine being displayed on the side.

These four pictures provide a brief insight into the origin growth and development of a successful shipping company in the second half of the twentieth century.

S A Vanguard (ex-*New Bern Victory*), 1945, 7,607 tons
The *S A Vanguard* was one of the three pioneering ships acquired in 1947, originally taking the name *Constantia*. She acquired the ponderous name *South African Vanguard* in 1961. This was reduced to 'S A' in 1966.

Originally built in Bethlehem (NJ) in 1945, she was sold to Panamanian interests in 1969, becoming the *Isabena*. She was wrecked off the coast of Pakistan in 1972.

In remarkably good condition for her age and origin, she is seen loading tinplate in Swansea's King's Dock.

South African Seafarer (ex-*Steenbok*, ex-*Clan Shaw*), 1950, 8,101 tons
The obvious connection with the British & Commonwealth group is seen here. One of a group of seven similar ships built by Greenock Dockyard for Clan Line and Pacific S. N., she was transferred to Bullard & King Line, eventually becoming the *Steenbok*. She was acquired by Safmarine in 1961.

She is seen entering Swansea Docks on a summer's evening in 1965. Sadly, while en route from Glasgow to Beira a year later she was wrecked off Cape Town, fortunately without loss of life.

S A Weltevreden, 1967, 10,545 tons
Built at Alblasserdam in the Netherlands, the large derrick was capable of lifting 125 tons. In 1975 she was modified in Japan, being fitted with extra holds and deck facilities for containers.

Transferred to Springbok Shipping as the *Safocean Weltevreden*, she was sold to Greek buyers in 1982. A sequence of further owner changes and periods of lay ups concluded with her being scrapped at Kaohsiung in 1988.

S A Sederburg, 1977, 52,615 tons

Within the space of thirty years, Safmarine became a major player in container shipping. The final response to containerisation was four state-of-the-art container ships that were built in France at Dunkerque. They had capacity for 2,450 TEUs, later increased to 2,500, of which 892 (later 1,110) were reefer containers. These fine ships also had accommodation for ten first-class passengers. They were originally known as the 'Big Whites' because of the way the tropical sun shone on their white hulls.

She survived the Maersk takeover, although she eventually lost her 'S A' prefix. She may also have been reflagged. After a useful life of thirty years, she was scrapped in 2008.

She is seen in Rotterdam in 1987.

Stanhope Steamship Company

The company was founded in London in 1934 by Jack Billmeir. It prospered through delivering cargo during the Spanish Civil War and by 1939 the company owned sixteen ships. Heavy losses were sustained during the Second World War.

By the early 1960s, the company was down to one ship. The company was sold when Jack Billmeir died in 1963.

Stanwear, 1956, 8,108 tons
Built by Wm Pickersgill, Sunderland, and taken over by George Nott of Coventry, she was renamed *Lady Era* in 1966 and was sold to Greek buyers in 1968. In 1977 she was wrecked off Port Cartier, Quebec. (Photograph courtesy of Stanhope S. S. Co. Ltd)

United States Lines, USA

United States Lines operated cargo liner services across the North Atlantic from 1921 until 1989. In the post-war era it relied largely on standard C2 class freighters until the introduction of the fast (24 knots) Challenger class in 1962. The company moved into containerisation in the late 1960s, but with overcapacity and deteriorating economic conditions the company was forced into bankruptcy on 24 November 1986, finally being liquidated by 1992.

American Scout, 1946, 8,228 tons
A standard C2, she was sold to Amercargo Shipping in 1969 to become the *Interscout*. While loading grain at Chittagong in October 1971 her cargo shifted, and she capsized and sank.
   One of my own shots captured her on a summer evening in Southampton in July 1966.

Departed Ambrose Light 0630 hrs. GMT, September 1, 1962

    Noon September 1 (1600 hrs GMT)
    Position 40.36 N. 68.54 W.
    Distance 225 miles. Speed 23.70 knots

    Noon September 2 (1500 hrs GMT)
    Position 44.05 N. 57.11 W.
    Distance 561 miles. Speed 24.39 knots

    Noon September 3 (1400 hrs GMT)
    Position 47.31 N. 44.40 W.
    Distance 564 miles. Speed 24.52 knots

    Noon September 4 (1300 hrs GMT)
    Position 49.52 N. 30.56 W.
    Distance 553 miles. Speed 24.05 knots

    Noon September 5 (1200 hrs GMT)
    Position 50.27 N. 16.12 W.
    Distance 573 miles. Speed 24.91 knots

Arrived at Le Havre Light vessel 1312 hrs GMT, September 6.

    TOTAL STEAMING TIME - AMBROSE LV TO HAVRE LV

        5 days: 6 hours: 42 minutes

        September 1 - 6, 1962.

        DISTANCE: 3101 miles

        AVERAGE SPEED: 24.47 knots

o————————oOo————————o

Above and left: American Challenger, 1962, 11,105 tons
Built at Newport News Dockyard, she was the first of a class of eleven fast (24-knot) cargo liners. On her maiden voyage to Europe she made a particularly fast crossing, averaging 24.42 knots. The log of the voyage is produced to the left.

To place this achievement in historical context, the Cunard Line entered a contract with the UK government, which required two fast (24 knots) mail liners. On her maiden eastbound voyage in 1907, the famous *Mauretania* took the Blue Riband at a similar speed.

She became the *Pioneer Moon* for US Lines' Pacific service and was eventually broken up in 1988. (Photograph and log entries courtesy of United States Lines)

Union-Castle Line

The Union-Castle Line came into being in December 1899 following the merger of the Union Line and the Castle Line, which were both operators on the England–South Africa run. By the mid-twentieth century it operated a fleet of twenty-seven ships consisting of mail liners and intermediate ships on the round Africa service, as well as cargo and reefer ships, all of which amounted to over 400,000 gross tons. In 1956 it merged with Clan Line to form British & Commonwealth Shipping. Shipping operations ended in 1977.

   Union-Castle did contribute to the collection, but the two ships present here have been acquired and chosen for special interest reasons.

Southampton Castle, 1965, 10,538 tons
Despite the long association with the port, this was a new name to the Union-Castle fleet. Built by Swan Hunter at Wallsend, and with twin diesel engines delivering over 34,000 shaft horse power, she and her sister were billed as the world's most powerful cargo liners. Two-screw ships, both were capable of 25 knots, although 27 knots were achieved on trials. They were designed to operate alongside the remaining mail ships.

   Accommodation for twelve passengers was added in 1967 when the service was diverted to include calls at St Helena and Ascension Island.

   Sold in 1978 to become the Italian *Franca C*, she became the Maltese *Franca* in 1983 before being broken up in Dalian in 1984.

Good Hope Castle, 1965, 10,538 tons
Like her sister the *Southampton Castle*, she was built by Swan Hunter at Wallsend. The original *Good Hope Castle* had been an Empire Chieftain class war standard that was scrapped in 1959. Like her sister, she was sold to the Italian Costa Line to become the *Paola C* and was also sold on to Maltese buyers in 1983 before being scrapped in Shanghai in 1984. (Copyright Harold Jordan postcards)

United Netherlands (VNSM), Netherlands

The company was formed after the First World War. Dutch shipping entrepreneurs saw a gap in the market as German companies had disappeared and demand was high. The directors of several existing Dutch shipping companies decided to establish a new company to fill the gap. The most notable gap was from Europe to East Africa, which was formerly operated by Deutsche Ost-Afrika Linie. Such a venture also presented competition to the British Union-Castle Line and British India Line. Operations were expanded to serve India by taking over services operated by Holland America Line (NASM), as well as to Australia by taking over Rotterdam Lloyd operations, and later to West Africa. Services to South Africa were reinforced by the acquisition of the newly formed and government-supported Holland South Africa Line (NZASM).

As such, the company was the Dutch equivalent of Union-Castle, the P&O British India Group and, to some extent, with its links to the Dutch East Indies, Alfred Holt's Blue Funnel Line.

To tackle the rising container revolution, the company merged with Royal Rotterdam Lloyd and other Dutch shipping companies in 1970 to form Nedlloyd, which eventually merged with P&O to form P&O Nedlloyd. In 2005 that company became part of the Danish Maersk Group.

Nijkerk, 1958, 6,579 tons
Built by De Noord in Alblasserdam, she survived the 1970 merger and was sold in 1977 to become the Singapore-flagged *Kota Sejati.*

Giessenkerk, 1956, 8,478 tons
Built by van der Giessen at Krimpen, she also survived the 1970 merger. She was sold in 1976 to become the *Mercury River* and again in 1977 to become the *Kota Sejarah*. She was scrapped at Gadani Beach in 1983.

Maaskerk (ex-*Tranquebar*, ex-*King's Point Victory*), 1945, 7,707 tons
Like most European shipping companies, VNSM had to acquire American standard Liberty and Victory tonnage immediately after the Second World War. However, this is something of a curiosity. A Victory ship built at the Bethlehem Fairfield yard in Baltimore (MD), she was sold initially to the Danish East Asiatic Line, becoming the *Tranquebar*. In 1955 she was purchased by VNSM. As part of the disposal programme of war standard tonnage, she was sold in 1966 to become the Liberian-flagged *Madonna* and was sold on again in 1969 before being scrapped at Kaohsiung in 1970.

Randfontein, 1958, 13,694 tons
The largest ship in the fleet, she was built by Wilton-Fijenoord at Schiedam. She had accommodation for both first- and tourist-class passengers. Swimming pool facilities were provided for both classes, which was unusual at the time.

Sold to Royal Interocean in 1971, she became the *Nieuw Holland* and was based in Hong Kong. In 1974 she became the Chinese *Yu Hua* and in 1981 the *Hai Xing*. Laid up in 1991, she was renamed *Herbert* in 1996 for her final voyage to the scrapyard at Alang.

Above: Sinoutskerk, 1962,
9,830 tons
One of nine 'S' class ships
built between 1960 and 1962,
she was built by Giessen
at Krimpen. In 1970 she
was lengthened and was
converted into a part container
ship. Renamed *Nedlloyd
Sinoutskerk* in 1977, she was
broken up at Kaohsiung in
December 1983.

Right: Westerkerk, 1967,
10,000 tons
This ship clearly exhibits a
serious response to the changing
conditions and advance of
containerisation. One of four fast
(21 knots) 'W' class ships, she
was built by Wilton-Fijenoord
and all ships were equipped with
a heavy-lift mast mounting a
120 ton derrick. All ships were
capable of carrying conventional
cargo and some containers.
Following the merger she was
renamed *Nedlloyd Westerkerk*
in 1977, although the prefix
was dropped in 1984. She was
broken up in Kaohsiung in
1987. (Photographs courtesy of
VNSM)

Zaankerk, 1957, 9,161 tons
Built by Howaldswerke in Hamburg, she was sold in 1978 to become the *Holystar* and was broken up in Cartagena in 1981.

United Steamship Company (Det Forende Dampskibs-Selskab A/S (DFDS)), Denmark

The company was formed from a number of smaller operations in 1866. It provided an important feeder service for emigrants from Scandinavia and the Baltic heading for the New World. It is still very active today, providing ferry and shipping services around the United Kingdom, the North Sea and the Baltic. Its containers are a familiar sight on Europe's roads and railways.

One of the more obliging features appreciated by ship spotters is the practice of painting the name in large letters along the side of the hull.

Colorado, 1958, 5,510 tons
Built as a cargo liner capable of carrying twelve passengers by Helsingørs Jernskibs & Maskinbyggeri of Helsingør in Eastern Denmark, she was sold along with her two sisters to the East African Shipping Line in 1968. She was renamed *Uganda* and flew the Ugandan flag. The company was not a success and following liquidation in 1980 the ship was sold initially to Panamanian buyers. After further changes of ownership and flag, she was eventually scrapped at Alang in 1988.

Maine, 1945, 3,541 tons
Built by Frederifkshavn, she was sold in 1966 to become the Greek *Hilde Manita*. She became the *Aghios Georgis* in 1970 and the *Lucky* in 1973. Her luck ran out when she was beached following a collision in the Lagos Roads in July 1975. (Postcards courtesy of DFDS)

Zim Israel Line

(Zim means fleets – see II Chronicles 9:21, Psalm 48:7, Isaiah 2:16 and other Old Testament references.)

Founded in 1945 by the Jewish Agency, the Histradut (Labour Foundation) and the Israel Maritime League in 1945, the first ship was purchased in 1947. Inevitably, that ship was involved in the post-war transportation of emigrants to the new state of Israel. During the 1948 war, the company's ships were vital to supplying the new state with food, freight and essential military equipment.

In the 1950s, Zim concentrated on passenger ships operating from Haifa in the Mediterranean to the United States. Now no longer in the passenger business, Zim still operate container services, and their ships and distinctive containers remain a familiar sight.

Jerusalem, 1957, 9,900 tons
The second Zim Line ship to carry the name, she was built in Germany as part of the Reparation Payments Agreement. From 1965 she was used exclusively for cruising and was chartered in 1966 to the Peninsular & Occidental Steamship Company, becoming the *Miami*.

She was sold in 1969 to Eastern Steamship to become the *New Bahama Star* and became the *Bahama Star* in 1972. She was sold again in 1975 to become the *Bonaire Star* and sank while under tow to the breakers in 1979.

Moledet, 1961, 6,306 tons
For the technical, the name means 'Fatherland' or perhaps 'Homeland'.

Built in France by Ateliers et Chantiers de Bretagne, she was sold to the Greek Epirotiki Lines to become the *Jupiter*. In October 1988, having just set out from Piraeus on an educational cruise, she was in collision with an Italian ship and sank. Mercifully, there were very few casualties.

Israel, 1955, 9,853 tons
Built by Deutsche Werft in Hamburg as part of the Repatriation Payments Agreement, she could accommodate 323 passengers, about 4,000 tons of cargo and, curiously, had a drive-in facility for about thirty cars.

Sold to Portugal in 1966 to become the *Amelia de Mello*, she was sold on to Greek buyers in 1972, becoming first the *Ithaca* and then the *Dolphin IV* in 1979. She was scrapped at Alang in 2003.

Zion, 1956, 9,855 tons
She was built by Deutsche Werft in Hamburg as part of the Reparation Payments Agreement to operate the Haifa–Piraeus–Naples–New York service. In 1966 she was sold to Portuguese buyers and was scrapped in 1974. (Postcards courtesy of Zim Israel Lines)